REDUCING GUN

VIOLENCE

Results from an Intervention in East Los Angeles

**GEORGE TITA • K. JACK RILEY • GREG RIDGEWAY
CLIFFORD GRAMMICH • ALLAN F. ABRAHAMSE
PETER W. GREENWOOD**

PREPARED FOR THE NATIONAL INSTITUTE OF JUSTICE

RAND
Public Safety and Justice

The research described in this report was conducted by RAND Public Safety and Justice for the National Institute of Justice under grant No. 98-LJ-CX-0043.

RAND is a nonprofit institution that helps improve policy and decisionmaking through research and analysis. RAND® is a registered trademark. RAND's publications do not necessarily reflect the opinions or policies of its research sponsors.

Cover design by Peter Soriano

Published 2003 by RAND
1700 Main Street, P.O. Box 2138, Santa Monica, CA 90407-2138
1200 South Hayes Street, Arlington, VA 22202-5050
201 North Craig Street, Suite 202, Pittsburgh, PA 15213-1516
RAND URL: http://www.rand.org/
To order RAND documents or to obtain additional information, contact Distribution Services: Telephone: (310) 451-7002; Fax: (310) 451-6915; Email: order@rand.org

This work of the RAND Public Safety and Justice program, made possible by a grant from the National Institute of Justice, is intended for a wide range of audiences, including professionals with interests in crime and violence reduction, interagency cooperation, and youthful offending. Although the book focuses on Los Angeles, its lessons are drawn in part from experience elsewhere and have implications for a broad range of communities.

The book extends a line of RAND research on developing strategic interventions to reduce violence. Other recent publications on this topic include

- George Tita, K. Jack Riley, and Peter W. Greenwood, "From Boston to Boyle Heights: The Process and Prospects of a 'Pulling Levers' Strategy in a Los Angeles Barrio," in Scott Decker, ed., *Policing Gangs and Youth Violence*, Belmont, Calif.: Wadsworth, 2003, pp. 102–130

- Peter W. Greenwood, Jeffrey Wasserman, Lois M. Davis, June A. Flora, Kim Ammann Howard, Nina Schleicher, Allan Abrahamse, Peter D. Jacobson, Grant Marshall, Carole Oken, Eric Larson, and James Chiesa, *The California Wellness Foundation's Violence Prevention Initiative: Findings from an Evaluation of the First Five Years*, Santa Monica, Calif.: RAND, MR-1342.0-TCWF, 2001

- Peter W. Greenwood, Karyn E. Model, C. Peter Rydell, and James Chiesa, *Diverting Children from a Life of Crime: Measuring Costs and Benefits*, Santa Monica, Calif.: RAND, MR-699-1-UCB/RC/IF, 1998.

CONTENTS

FIGURES

TABLES

Violent crime, especially gun homicide, is concentrated in particular locations and populations. It affects cities more than other areas of the United States and is more likely to be committed by and against young males. Within cities, both violent crime and gun homicide by youths are concentrated in neighborhoods with high levels of poverty, drug dealing, and/or gang activity.

One recent response to this concentration of violence has been the Boston Gun Project, formed by a coalition of researchers, community leaders, criminal justice agency representatives, and clergy who researched, designed, implemented, and monitored a project to reduce youth violence by reducing gang and gun violence. Shortly after the launch of the project in 1996, youth homicide fell by about two-thirds in that city.

The Boston experience led the National Institute of Justice (NIJ) to fund RAND to assess whether the process used to reduce gun violence by youths in Boston could be adapted elsewhere. Specifically, the charter was to select an area with a violent crime problem that was amenable to an intervention, analyze the composition of the violence to identify strategies that would address the problem and the resources needed to do so, develop an intervention from among the strategies and resources that was tailored to the composition of the problem, implement the intervention, and evaluate its effect. The Los Angeles Police Department Hollenbeck area—a 15-square-mile area east of downtown Los Angeles that encompasses a population of approximately 200,000 and the communities of El Sereno, Lincoln Heights, and Boyle Heights—was chosen for the replication. Although the Hollenbeck project was expected to use the basic procedures of the Boston project, particularly leadership by a working group that brought together community leaders, it was also expected that the type of problems addressed and the nature of the intervention might differ from those in Boston, especially given the greater decentralization of criminal justice authorities in Los Angeles.

Crime in the Hollenbeck area is especially violent and involves disproportionate numbers of youths. Reported property crime rates in the area are among the lowest in the city, but the area ranks at or near the top in rates of violent crime, including homicide. Our crime analysis demonstrated, contrary to the perception of some, that little of this violence was related to battles between gangs over control of drug markets. Rather, inter-gang violence more typically dealt with personal or gang honor or prestige. Although its gangs are among the oldest in the city, the area had not previously had a special intervention to combat violence, such as the one the NIJ asked RAND to investigate.

After the Hollenbeck working group was convened, it spent several months considering a plan to quell gang violence in the wake of any triggering event that might lead one gang to retaliate against another. Because the violence was gang-driven, the working group designed a strategy and intervention that leveraged the collective structure of the gang. Among other features, the plan was to include

- increased Los Angeles Police Department (LAPD) patrols in the immediate geographic area of the triggering event

- deployment of officers from specialized police units to the broader neighborhood and additional police patrols in public parks

- more-stringent enforcement of housing codes for properties used by gang members and of public housing eligibility rules prohibiting possession of drugs, firearms, and other contraband

- more-stringent enforcement of parole and probation conditions and serving of outstanding warrants on gang members who had committed prior offenses

- referral of gun law violations to federal prosecutors

- dynamic and rapid application of these intervention elements after each violent incident to ensure that perpetrators and victims understood there were consequences for violent behavior.

A brazen "walk-by" gang shooting and resulting double homicide in early October 2000 triggered implementation of the planned intervention in Boyle Heights in the southern portion of the Hollenbeck area. Just prior to this event, community-based organizations responsible for incentives to prevent violence had argued for immediate implementation of sanctions or the law enforcement components of the intervention because of escalating violent crime in the area.

The intervention differed from what was planned in that it was not dynamic. That is, although the intervention was implemented as planned against the first incident, working group members did not constantly reprioritize and reallocate resources after each violent incident but instead focused their efforts almost exclusively on the two gangs involved in the triggering incident and their immediate neighborhoods. Also, the social services that accompanied the Boston initiative were never consistently or widely available in the Hollenbeck intervention, reflecting both the decision to proceed with law enforcement sanctions before social service incentives were in place and the very long time needed to build additional capacity for such social services as job training.

In assessing the effects of the intervention, RAND researchers sought to answer three questions, specifically whether the intervention helped to reduce

- violent crime: homicides, attempted homicides, robberies, assaults, and kidnappings

- gang crime: violent crime and terrorist threats, firearm discharge, vandalism, and graffiti committed by gang members

- gun crime: any of the above crimes that involved use of a firearm.

The analysis compared changes in crime for three periods across three comparison areas. The three time periods were the six months prior to the triggering event—the *pre-intervention* period; the four months in which all parts of the intervention were applied—the *sup-*

pression period; and the two months in which only selected parts of the intervention were applied, such as heightened patrol of public housing units in the area and greater enforcement of probation and parole regulations—the *deterrence* period. The three comparison areas were (1) Boyle Heights compared with the remainder of the Hollenbeck area, (2) the five police reporting districts where the intervention was targeted compared with the remainder of Boyle Heights, and (3) the Census block groups comprising the turf of the targeted gangs compared with a group of Census block groups scattered throughout Hollenbeck that most closely matched the characteristics of the targeted area.

In Boyle Heights, gang crime decreased significantly compared with other regions of Hollenbeck during the suppression period of the intervention, and violent, gang, and gun crime all decreased significantly in the deterrence period. The data suggest that the significant reduction in gang crime may have begun in the suppression period. Violent crime, however, did not decrease significantly in the suppression period.

In the five targeted police reporting districts, violent crime decreased significantly in comparison with the rest of Boyle Heights in the suppression and the deterrence periods, and gang crime decreased significantly in the suppression period. Neither gang crime in the deterrence period nor gun crime in the deterrence or suppression periods decreased significantly in comparison with the remainder of Boyle Heights, although the generally low number of gun crimes in the targeted reporting districts makes it difficult to detect significant changes.

In the Census block groups overlapping the targeted reporting districts, violent crime decreased significantly compared with the matched blocks. The data suggest that some of this significant reduction may have persisted into the deterrence period. Gang and gun crime did not decrease significantly, although low numbers of these crimes made it difficult to detect significant changes.

In addition to the above formal analyses of the effects of the intervention, RAND researchers examined the effects of the intervention on neighboring areas and gangs. The intervention did not displace crime from the targeted areas and gangs to others; rather, crime decreased in surrounding communities as well.

The replication of the Boston process in Hollenbeck succeeded in that it used data analysis to identify both problems and potential interventions and led a working group like the one in Boston to implement a well-designed intervention that helped reduce gang crime and violent crime in the targeted area. It also succeeded in getting decentralized criminal justice organizations to focus their unique and often disparate resources on a problem in a single area. Community support for the intervention was also high, in large part because of the inclusion of community representatives in the working group process.

Nevertheless, the intervention was not implemented as designed, and it never developed dynamically or in response to changing needs. Part of the reason stems from the reorganization of LAPD gang crime units in response to a scandal involving some gang unit officers who planted evidence and used excessive force. Also, the project did not succeed in getting working group participants, who referred to it as the "RAND study" or the "RAND project," to view it as their own and seek to continue it. No single agency emerged to take charge of the project and carry it forward, perhaps because of limited resources for the work.

For future projects such as this one to work beyond a trial period, city leaders need to establish processes to support, and hold accountable, agencies in such collaboration. Such efforts would require more information on project costs than was gathered by this effort, which, like similar efforts, focused almost exclusively on measuring the project's effects on crime reduction. Only with the collection of cost information can a final evaluation be made of whether the effort was worthwhile.

This work, like the Hollenbeck Operation Ceasefire it evaluates, would not have been possible without the participation of colleagues and friends in the Los Angeles Police Department, the Los Angeles County Department of Probation, the Los Angeles County District Attorney's office, the U.S. Attorney's office, the Los Angeles City Attorney's office, the City of Los Angeles Housing Authority, the Los Angeles office of the U.S. Department of Housing and Urban Development, the Los Angeles County Unified School District Police, Soledad Enrichment Action, Homeboy Industries/Jobs for a Future, the East Los Angeles Community Development Corporation, the Boyle Heights Chamber of Commerce, the Association of Community Based Gang Intervention Workers, the East Los Angeles Deanery of the Catholic Archdiocese of Los Angeles, Delores Mission, and White Memorial Medical Center. In all, more than 100 people from these organizations helped us think about reducing gun violence. None of them were compensated for their assistance, save for the occasional lunches of delicious Mexican food provided at strategy sessions by the staff of Resurrection Catholic Parish.

We acknowledge the assistance of several RAND colleagues who helped this research at various stages. Joe Hendrickson, Barbara Panitch, and Siddhartha Khosla assisted in field contacts and gathering data at various points in the project. We also acknowledge the contributions of Jonathan Zasloff, now at the UCLA School of Law, during the early stages of this project.

We are also thankful to our reviewers—John Engberg (RAND), Jeffrey Grogger (UCLA), and two anonymous National Institute of Justice reviewers—for their comments. Because these reviewers were not part of the project team, they were able to have an independent perspective on our analysis. This independent review is an important part of our quality assurance process.

LAPD	Los Angeles Police Department
NIJ	National Institute of Justice
OCB	Operations Central Bureau
RD	reporting district
TMC	The Mob Crew

Chapter One

REDUCING GUN VIOLENCE IN URBAN AREAS

Violent crime, especially gun homicide, is concentrated in particular locations and populations. It affects cities more than other areas of the United States and is more likely to be committed by and against young males. Within cities, both violent crime and gun homicide by youths are concentrated in neighborhoods with high levels of poverty, drug dealing, and/or gang activity.

One recent response to this concentration of violence was the Boston Gun Project, also known as Operation Ceasefire, formed by a coalition of Boston-based researchers, community leaders, criminal justice agency representatives, and clergy who researched, designed, implemented, and monitored a project to reduce youth violence by reducing gang and gun violence. Key to this project was a dynamic combination of sanctions (e.g., stricter enforcement of parole and probation regulations) and incentives for prevention (e.g., job training and substance abuse treatment), or a combination of sanctions and services that changed as conditions warranted. Shortly after the launch of the project in 1996, homicides committed by youths fell by about two-thirds in that city.

Could the Boston Gun Project be adapted so as to reduce violent crime in other urban areas? To answer this question, RAND, with support from the National Institute of Justice, sought to replicate the Boston initiative to Los Angeles, or to develop, test, and evaluate strategies for reducing gun violence among youth in a different setting. Although the Los Angeles project was expected to include the basic elements of the Boston project, particularly leadership by a working group that brought together community leaders, it was also

1

expected that the type of problems addressed and the nature of the intervention might differ from those in Boston, given the greater decentralization of criminal justice authorities in Los Angeles.[1]

At first, it was unclear whether such an approach could be replicated in Los Angeles. Los Angeles' economy and government, unlike those of many northern and eastern cities such as Boston, are relatively decentralized, with points of political leverage being particularly dispersed. There were also concerns—given both the long history of successful innovation in local law enforcement and the more recent scandals affecting the Los Angeles Police Department (LAPD) and subsequent calls for reform leading to greater insularity on the part of some law enforcement personnel—whether Los Angeles area law enforcement officials would welcome interventions developed elsewhere. Finally, it was also unclear whether an intervention designed for predominantly African American gangs in Boston would be suitable for adaptation or application in what is becoming a predominantly Latino city. At the same time, given the links between youth gun violence and gang violence in Los Angeles,[2] it was clear that any intervention designed to address youth violence would have to address gang violence in some way. Although community leaders who became involved in the ultimate project continually cautioned that "[L.A.] isn't Boston," suggesting in particular that L.A. gangs were "bigger and badder" than those in Boston, they also came to see, as they learned more about the new initiative, that some new approach to gang violence might be fruitful given the failure of myriad approaches to the problem in Los Angeles in recent decades.

The effort to select a Los Angeles intervention site began in the summer of 1998. While the Boston Gun Project was implemented citywide, a citywide application was obviously impractical in Los Angeles given its enormous size. Hence, the researchers sought to identify a smaller intervention area within the city or county. A snowball-sampling framework, in which initial potential working group members were asked to identify additional members, was

---

[1] For a more thorough description of the Los Angeles project and its origins, see Tita, Riley, and Greenwood, 2003. For more on the origins of the Boston Gun Project, see Kennedy, Piehl, and Braga, 1996.

[2] For a discussion of gangs' contributions to homicide in Los Angeles, see Vigil, 1988; Vigil and Yun, 1990; and Maxson and Klein, 1996.

used to assemble a working group for the project. Six persons attended the first prospective working group meeting for the project in early 1999: two from RAND, three from the LAPD, and one from the Los Angeles County Probation Department. After discussing the merits and goals of the project, these six participants identified other individuals and agencies as partners for the project.

Originally, Van Nuys, an area in the San Fernando Valley plagued by relatively high homicide rates, blight, and widespread drug dealing, was considered as a possible site for the intervention, but it was rejected because another program designed to control gang behavior was already in place there.[3] Ultimately, the LAPD Hollenbeck area—a 15-square-mile area east of downtown Los Angeles that encompasses a population of approximately 200,000 and the communities of El Sereno, Lincoln Heights, and Boyle Heights—within the Central Bureau area was chosen for the replication (Figure 1.1).[4] Because no other programs against gang violence, such as that in Van Nuys, were in place in Hollenbeck during the time of this research, the area offered an opportunity to isolate and assess the effects of the proposed intervention.

Hollenbeck gangs are among the oldest in the city, with some intergenerational gangs tracing their roots back to before World War II.[5] Hollenbeck has an 81 percent Latino majority, primarily comprising persons of Mexican heritage. In fact, the area has had a Latino majority for many years, unlike other Los Angeles areas with gang problems where the population has changed from a black majority to a Latino majority in recent years. There is a unique pattern to crime in Hollenbeck. As elsewhere in the city and nation, homicide rates in Hollenbeck peaked in the early 1990s; since then, the area has had a higher homicide rate than both Los Angeles and the nation (Figure 1.2). Yet while Hollenbeck in recent years has consistently ranked

---

[3]For more on the Van Nuys interventions see Grogger, 2002, and Maxson, Hennigan, and Sloane, 2003.

[4]The LAPD is perhaps the only entity to consider this area as a whole and to call it "Hollenbeck." Geographically, the LAPD is organized into four Bureaus—Central, South, Valley, and West—with four or five Community Areas comprising each Bureau area. Hollenbeck is one of five Community Areas in the Central Bureau area.

[5]For more on one of the oldest gangs in the area and the city, White Fence, see Moore, 1978; for more on other long-time gangs in the area, see, among others, Vigil, 1988.

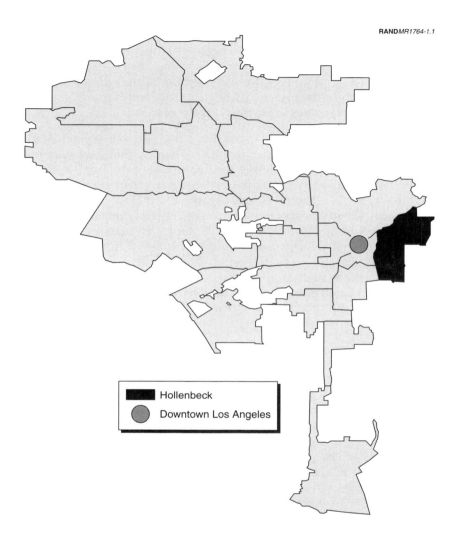

RAND*MR1764-1.1*

Figure 1.1—LAPD Area Boundaries

among the top three or four of the 18 policing areas in violent crime, it ranks near the bottom in reported property crimes. Detectives knowledgeable about property crime in the area contend that it is more likely to be committed by a large transient population, many

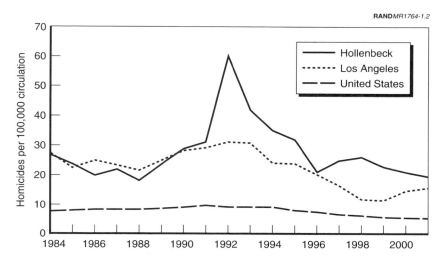

RAND*MR1764-1.2*

SOURCE: Federal Bureau of Investigation, *Crime in the United States*, annual;
Los Angeles Police Department, *Statistical Digest*, annual.

**Figure 1.2—Homicide Rates in Hollenbeck, Los Angeles, and the United
States, 1984–2001**

of whom are addicted to narcotics, than by gang members who are
instead much more likely to be overrepresented in violent crime.

Analysis of incidents of homicide and gun violence in Hollenbeck did
indeed demonstrate that gangs were at the core of those problems.
From a detailed analysis of Hollenbeck homicide files, we found that
gang issues, including disputes over gang turf and "respect," were
the precipitating motive for half of the nearly 200 homicides that occurred in Hollenbeck between 1995 and 1998. An additional one-
quarter of Hollenbeck homicides involved gang members, but the
motivation was tied to such factors as arguments, drug debts, or
domestic altercations. Only about one-fifth of all Hollenbeck homicides had a drug motive or involved a dispute over drug debts, the
quantity or quality of drugs, or the robbery of a drug dealer. Very few
of the drug-involved homicides were motivated by disputes over
drug sales territory.

Preliminary findings indicating that relatively few gang homicides in Hollenbeck involved drug dealing drew incredulous responses from members of the working group, including one law enforcement member who insisted "these kids are . . . being killed because of [dope]." Nevertheless, careful reanalysis of the homicide data confirmed these findings and pointed to an important distinction confirmed by other research. While gang members may sell drugs and may kill and are killed selling drugs, the motivation for these homicides is not likely to stem from gangs fighting for market control. Other researchers have similarly contended that the links between youth gangs, drugs, and violence have been overdrawn (Howell and Decker, 1999). In an analysis of Chicago gang homicides, Block and Block (1993) reported that few gang-on-gang homicides involved disputes over drug markets but found that Latino gang members in particular are likely to engage in expressive acts of violence (e.g., defense of gang honor or personal status). Similar findings have been documented in Pittsburgh (Cohen and Tita, 1999), St. Louis (Rosenfeld, Bray, and Egley, 1999), and Boston (Kennedy, 1997).

Other aspects of Hollenbeck gang violence offered promising points for an intervention. Analysis of gang activity showed each gang concentrated within its own turf and its violence against others typically consisting of premeditated attacks against members of other gangs in their rivals' territories.[6] In other words, because gang violence was spatially concentrated, it could perhaps be addressed by focusing an intervention on a small area, maybe one comprising no more than several square blocks. An anti-gang initiative based on the Boston model might succeed by concentrating its resources, particularly its law enforcement elements, on such a small area, although some elements of the intervention, particularly any social services that might accompany it, would, by their diffuse nature, also affect a broader area.

In this document, we evaluate how well the adaptation of the Boston initiative to Hollenbeck worked in curbing violence and gang crime there. Chapter Two discusses the Hollenbeck area and the initiative there in more detail. Chapter Three presents a statistical analysis of the effects of the initiative in reducing violence and gang crime in

---

[6]For more on predatory gun violence by gangs, see Tita and Griffiths, 2003.

Hollenbeck. We conclude in Chapter Four by discussing the implications of the analysis for other community initiatives against gun violence.

Chapter Two

IMPLEMENTING THE HOLLENBECK INITIATIVE

DESIGNING THE INITIATIVE

The Hollenbeck initiative was designed by a working group that eventually included nearly a score of law enforcement, community-based, and faith-based organizations and institutions (Table 2.1). As the Boston project had, the Hollenbeck initiative quickly came to draw upon support of area churches, including those in the East Los Angeles Deanery of the Catholic Archdiocese. In the first meeting of the working group within Hollenbeck, for example, 14 of the 17 persons in attendance were priests from area parishes. More generally, there is a long tradition of classic, gang-based "street intervention" in the area.[1] Homeboy Industries/Jobs for a Future, a local employment referral center established by a Jesuit priest and driven by the principle that "nothing stops a bullet like a job," provides social services and job opportunities to youth in the region.

Having this community structure for information and support was vital to the acceptance of any gun violence strategy that might include law enforcement elements, given concern that any new initiative not rely exclusively on suppression of gang activities, as past interventions throughout Los Angeles had. RAND personnel regularly met with this group to discuss their research on Hollenbeck, its implications for anti-violence policy options, and the work of each participant in following these options. The working group

---

[1]For historical descriptions of gang workers in this community, see Moore, 1978; Vigil, 1988; and Vigil, 1990.

Table 2.1

Agencies Participating in Hollenbeck Initiative

Criminal Justice	Community-Based	Faith-Based/Other
Los Angeles Police Department	Soledad Enrichment Action	Catholic Archdiocese of Los Angeles, East Los Angeles Deanery
Los Angeles County Department of Probation	Homeboy Industries/Jobs for a Future	Delores Mission
California Division of Corrections (Parole)	East Los Angeles Community Development Corporation	White Memorial Medical Center
California Youth Authority (Juvenile Parole)	Boyle Heights Chamber of Commerce	
U.S. Attorney's Office	Mothers of East L.A.	
Los Angeles County District Attorney	Local parent-teacher organizations	
Los Angeles City Attorney	The Association of Community Based Gang Intervention Workers	
City of Los Angeles Housing Authority		
Los Angeles Unified School District Police		

sought to pursue a policy that balanced "sticks" and "carrots," or law enforcement responses with prevention and social intervention programs. The goal was simple: Increase the cost of violent behavior to gang members while increasing the benefits of nonviolent behavior.

As noted in the preceding chapter, the spatial concentration of gang activity made both the design of an intervention and the selection of focus points easier. The complicated network of rivalries among the 29 "criminally active street gangs" (the term used by the LAPD to describe problematic, violent groups), while difficult to disrupt completely, offered several points for intervention (Figure 2.1).

RAND*MR1764-2.1*

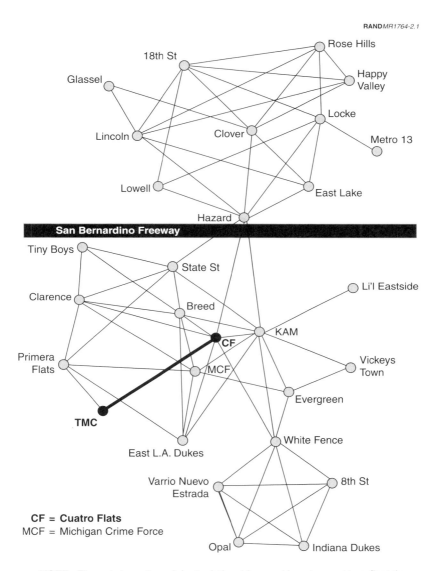

NOTE: Figure is based on violent relationships, and is not meant to reflect the geographic distribution of gangs.

Figure 2.1—Network Map of Hollenbeck Gang Rivalries

Our spatial and network analysis of area gangs indicated an important structural break in the neighborhood that allowed for a natural experiment. The San Bernardino Freeway (Interstate Highway 10) divides Hollenbeck into north and south sections. With one minor exception, no gang has any rivalries that cross the freeway. We chose to focus the intervention in the southern portion of Hollenbeck, called Boyle Heights, because this was where most violent crime (59 percent of all Hollenbeck violent crimes in the six months prior to the intervention) and the most intense gang rivalries were, and to compare the results of the intervention with trends in crime elsewhere in the area.

In our study of gangs, we learned that not all gang members are violent and not all gangs are violent. Nevertheless, most gangs have some sort of hierarchy that includes "shot callers," or leaders who tend to be older and more isolated from day-to-day activity of the gang; "shooters," or those most likely to commit an attack against another gang; and "active soldiers," or those most likely to associate with a gang but not necessarily involved in attacking rivals. Most gang members are in the latter group.

Initially, the intervention was to be targeted at shot callers and shooters, who were thought to be most vulnerable to the pressures that could be brought to bear by more stringent law enforcement targeted at persons with outstanding warrants or parole and probation violations. Nevertheless, vulnerability profiles compiled for four key Boyle Heights gangs found only nine of these gang leaders (or fewer than one in four) with outstanding warrants, and only four for whom bail had been set at $5,000 or higher. By contrast, there were 68 other members of these four gangs with outstanding warrants, and 29 for whom bail had been set at $5,000 or higher. A similar pattern existed for probation and parole conditions. These analyses also revealed a gap in the direct leverage over young gang members. Very few of the youngest gang members, whom gang intelligence detectives indicated were disproportionately responsible for gang violence, had any kind of official history or points of leverage available; i.e., they did not yet have extensive criminal records and were therefore less vulnerable to more stringent enforcement of warrants or of parole and probation regulations.

Because of the large number of persons across all gangs with vulnerabilities to more-stringent law enforcement measures, the working group therefore designed an intervention based on the Boston model of "collective accountability"—one seeking to hold all members of a gang accountable for the act of any individual member. Primary points of leverage for holding other gang members accountable after an individual gang member committed a violent act were to include

- more-stringent enforcement of parole and probation conditions[2] and serving of outstanding warrants on gang members who had committed prior offenses

- increased LAPD patrols in the territory of the offending gang

- more-stringent enforcement of public housing residency requirements for properties used by gang members, including prohibitions of drugs, firearms, and other contraband

- referral of gun law violations to federal prosecutors.

Additional secondary points of leverage designed to quell gang violence in the wake of any gang attack upon another were to include

- increased LAPD patrols in the immediate geographic area of the incident

- deployment of officers from specialized police units to the broader area

- additional police patrols in public parks

---

[2]Typical probation conditions in California include agreeing to permit probation and peace officers to search one's person and property at any time of day or night without warrant or probable cause; not use or possess narcotics, dangerous or restricted drugs, or associated paraphernalia; stay away from places where drug users, buyers, or sellers congregate; not associate with persons known to be narcotic or drug users or sellers; not associate with known gang members; keep probation officer advised of residence at all times; not own, use, or possess any dangerous or deadly weapons.

The reader might question why such provisions are not always stringently enforced. The answer lies in the caseload that each probation officer must carry. The number of county probation officers remains at the level of about 25 years ago, while the number of parole and probation cases each officer must handle has doubled, to about 300 cases per officer. See Tita, Riley, and Greenwood (2003), particularly pp. 116–117.

- installation of traffic barriers and other physical features to improve neighborhood quality of life

- more-stringent area enforcement of vehicle and housing codes

- collection of support payments for those gang members with children and enforcement of truancy laws for those who were underage.

Many agencies working on points of leverage to hold gang members accountable for individual actions were also to offer prevention and intervention programs (Table 2.2). Parole officers and city agencies, for example, were to offer job training and development opportunities, and probation officers were to offer access to tattoo removal and substance abuse treatment. Other area agencies were also to offer similar services; an area hospital, for example, was to offer tattoo removal and substance abuse treatment programs, while Homeboy Industries/Jobs for a Future was also to offer tattoo removal and job training and development services.

The intervention, to be known as Operation Ceasefire (a name also used to describe the Boston initiative), was to be implemented in the wake of a triggering event, or immediately after a gang member committed a violent act and law enforcement officials had reasonable certainty about the perpetrator and his gang.[3] Prior to the intervention, there was considerable "retailing the message"—by Homeboy Industries, local police, and Catholic parishes—spreading the news about the pending implementation, including the consequences that would result from violent behavior and the availability of services and alternatives to violent behavior.

IMPLEMENTING THE INTERVENTION

By design, the prevention efforts were to be coupled tightly with the primary and secondary levers of law enforcement responses, and

---

[3]Reasonable certainty could stem from knowledge about the victim's adversaries, especially in other gangs, and reports from witnesses about gang slogans shouted before the attack. The standard of reasonable certainty was not the same as probable cause for arrest, but many of the levers designed, such as more-stringent enforcement of parole and probation regulations requiring subjects to agree to be searched in a wide variety of circumstances, did not require such an exacting standard for implementation.

Table 2.2

Intervention Levers and Components

Agency	Primary Levers	Secondary Levers	Prevention Services
Parole officers	Enforcement of parole regulations		Access to job training and development
Probation officers	Enforcement of probation regulations		Access to tattoo removal; substance abuse treatment
LAPD	Warrant enforcement, saturation patrol, drug market abatement		
Housing police	Enforcement of public housing residency re-quirements	Property code enforcement	
Hospital			Tattoo removal; substance abuse treatment
Homeboy Industries/ Jobs for a Future			Tattoo removal; job training and development
Various city agencies		Child support payment enforcement; property code enforcement	Job training and development

prevention was key to attracting community input to, and support for, the intervention. The events of the implementation, however, prevented the planned coupling of these services.

At an early October 2000 meeting to discuss implementation of the initiative, representatives of community organizations, who were to offer prevention and intervention programs as part of the initiative and were the greatest supporters of those programs, urged that the law enforcement elements of the initiative be implemented immediately. They noted that it did not appear possible to coordinate their services with law enforcement interventions, given the long lead time needed to marshal resources to increase the capacity of local social service providers. In the meantime, they argued, violent crime was perceived to be escalating rapidly in the area, and events involving two gangs in particular, TMC (a.k.a. The Mob Crew) and Cuatro Flats (note highlighted link in Figure 2.1), were so troubling that they should be given the highest level of attention immediately. The local LAPD captain attending the meeting agreed the intervention should be launched after one final review through his chain of command.

The following weekend, a brazen "walk-by" shooting occurred in the heart of TMC territory. Five Cuatro Flats members exited a van driven by a female associate, ran around the nearby corner, and opened fire on a group of TMC members in front of a known TMC member's home. After the shooting, two persons were dead: a 19-year-old TMC member in the direct line of fire and a 10-year-old child who had been riding her scooter down the street and was killed by a stray bullet. This became the triggering event for Operation Ceasefire, which was launched the next day.

The LAPD quickly allocated additional resources to the known territories of both Cuatro Flats, the offending gang, and TMC, the victimized gang (Figure 2.2). It increased patrols within the five reporting districts (RDs) near the site of the homicides and in Cuatro Flats or TMC territory and deployed police officers from specialized units to the area, including Metro Unit (which includes the SWAT team used throughout the city), the Operations Central Bureau (OCB) Special Enforcement Unit (similar to Metro, but deployed only in the areas comprising the Central Bureau), and the OCB Traffic Bureau. Each weekend for the next two months, two officers on horseback patrolled the local parks and the adjacent public housing development within the targeted area. Housing Police also increased patrol of the Pico Gardens Housing Development, a hotbed of Cuatro Flats activities.

The Hollenbeck area gang detective unit documented vulnerabilities of members in both gangs, and, in late October 2000, LAPD, Housing Police, and probation officers visited the last-known residences of

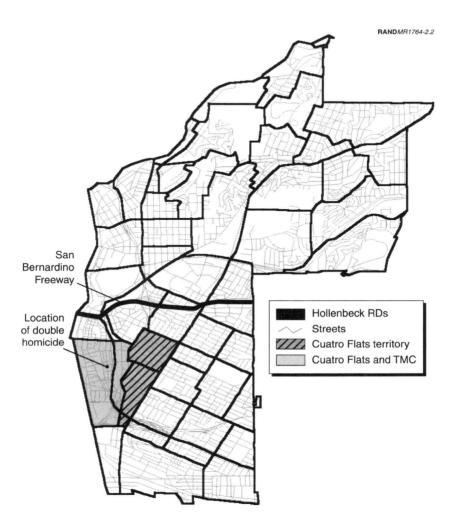

RAND*MR1764-2.2*

San
Bernardino
Freeway

Location
of double
homicide

	Hollenbeck RDs
	Streets
	Cuatro Flats territory
	Cuatro Flats and TMC

**Figure 2.2—Hollenbeck Reporting Districts (RDs), Cuatro Flats and TMC
Territories, and Location of Double Homicide Triggering Intervention**

eight Cuatro Flats gang members, arresting three for outstanding
warrants or probation violations and confiscating small amounts of
marijuana from two residences, although they found no illegal guns.

At each residence, officers made clear that their actions were a direct result of the violence committed by members of the Cuatro Flats gang. Over the next three months, these officers also paid visits to nearly two dozen other members of both gangs, which resulted in five additional arrests or revocations of parole. They also seized illegal guns at five locations and found four instances where there was sufficient evidence to refer a gun case to the U.S. Attorney's office for prosecution.

Beyond the intermediate actions taken against members of the two gangs involved in the triggering event, several other secondary interventions were taken. The city attorney orchestrated inspections from health and child welfare agencies at properties where gang members congregated and increased attention to specific buildings and housing units in TMC territory. Within two weeks of the event, an L.A. city council member helped get speed bumps installed and the alleyway behind the site of the triggering event fenced off, making future attacks and escape more difficult. Community leaders also sought to help police develop information on the triggering attack committed by Cuatro Flats gang members and earlier incidents involving TMC members, ultimately posting a $5,000 reward through the assistance of a member of the county board of supervisors.

INTENDED AND ACTUAL INTERVENTION

The intervention as implemented differed in several ways from the intervention as planned. As noted previously, the prevention and social intervention programs and services were not consistently or widely available, in part because of the decision prior to the triggering event to launch the law enforcement portion of Operation Ceasefire as soon as possible.

More generally, the intervention was not dynamic. That is, the working group members did not constantly reprioritize and reallocate resources after each violent incident, but rather focused almost exclusively on the two gangs involved in the triggering incident. For example, additional shootings involving other gangs that occurred in the week after the triggering incident did not receive additional intervention associated with Operation Ceasefire. One consequence of the focus on the single triggering event was that the intervention never created a consistent perception that violent behavior would provoke an immediate response. Thus, the intervention became even more spatially concentrated. That is, rather than operating throughout Boyle Heights, the intervention became concentrated in the five reporting districts where the TMC and Cuatro Flats gangs were most active.

Nevertheless, in the aftermath of the intervention, violent and gang crime did decrease in the targeted area, as well as in other areas of Boyle Heights and in Hollenbeck. In the next chapter, we present a formal statistical analysis to identify the areas in which the intervention may have been most effective, before discussing, in the final chapter, the implications of this initiative for future adaptations.

Chapter Three

EVALUATING THE INITIATIVE

All elements of the initiative were targeted at the five reporting districts near the site of the triggering event. Some elements of the initiative, such as "retailing" of its message as well as its social services and other community engagement programs, were targeted more broadly throughout Boyle Heights. The balance of Hollenbeck, or that part of Hollenbeck north of the San Bernardino Freeway, received no intervention.

These varying intervention levels present three geographic comparisons for determining the effectiveness of the initiative in reducing violent crime, gang crime, and gun crime. The comparisons include the following:

- Boyle Heights compared with the remainder of Hollenbeck— Hollenbeck south of the San Bernardino Freeway compared with that portion north of it. The strength of this comparison is that the two areas are well matched in several characteristics. They receive the same basic policing and social services and they are somewhat isolated. The weakness of the comparison is that the intervention was only partially implemented in Boyle Heights as a whole; the portion that was implemented throughout Boyle Heights, "retailing" of its message and associated social services, would need to have a very strong effect to be seen as significant in statistical analysis of crime trends.

- Targeted reporting districts (RDs) compared with the remainder of Boyle Heights—those areas where all parts of the intervention were implemented compared with those areas where only select portions of the intervention were implemented. The strength of this comparison is that it isolates the impact of the law enforcement interventions. The weakness of this comparison is that the five targeted RDs were among the most likely in Boyle Heights to be the site of a violent crime, and therefore these RDs may not be truly comparable to the rest of Boyle Heights.

- Specific Census block groups within the targeted RDs compared with matched Census block groups elsewhere in Boyle Heights— those areas where all parts of the intervention were most focused compared with area Census block groups matched on key characteristics such as crime and poverty rates. The advantage of this comparison is that it focuses on comparing the targeted area with a portion of Hollenbeck more like it than is the remainder of Boyle Heights, thereby providing a more targeted assessment of the likely effects of the intervention. The weakness of this comparison is that the absolute number of observations (or number of crimes) in such a small area is relatively small, making it more difficult to find statistically significant differences.

Unlike evaluation efforts of the Boston Gun Project, we do not make any comparisons between Los Angeles and other cities. The Boston initiative was implemented citywide; therefore, comparing changes in levels of violence in Boston to those in other northeastern cities was appropriate (see Braga et al., 2001). The Los Angeles adaptation was limited to only a small portion of the city. To conduct inter-city comparisons, we would have had to identify relevant or similar neighborhoods within other cities and then control for variation within and between cities. This did not seem to be an appropriate analytic approach. Similarly, given the unique characteristics of Hollenbeck noted earlier, including the unique structure of its gang problem, we did not believe there were appropriate comparison neighborhoods within Los Angeles.

DIMENSIONS AND EFFECTS

In assessing the effects of the intervention, we sought to answer three questions, specifically, whether the intervention might have been associated with reductions in the following:

- Violent crime: the number of homicides, attempted homicides, robberies, assaults, and kidnappings

- Gang crime: violent crime and terror threats, firearm discharge, vandalism, and graffiti committed by gang members

- Gun crime: including any of the above crimes that involved use of a firearm.

To address these questions, we used data from two different LAPD files. The first includes all violent crime incidents. The second includes violent crimes and other incidents in which the victim or offender is known to be a victim of a gang. Both files also contain detailed information on weapon used, if any, in the crime.

As with any evaluation relying on official police data, our data are subject to a reporting bias. Because the analysis was conducted within a region policed by the same agency, however, we view non-reporting to be a random variable that does not differ systematically among the various neighborhoods within Hollenbeck. Furthermore, there is no reason to believe that reporting behaviors of the population would change before, during, or after the evaluation period. Even if they did, they would likely do so in a way that biased our results downward or understated the effectiveness of the intervention. That is, area residents may have been more inclined to report crimes after the intervention, generating more observations for our analysis and presenting an illusion of increasing numbers of crimes. Similarly, the greater presence of police officers in the area could have generated more crime reports (or observations for our analysis) simply because there were more police to observe illegal behavior. Broader trends in crime in Hollenbeck as a whole and throughout the city and nation could also theoretically confound our results, although decreasing numbers of homicides since 1999 in Hollenbeck and increasing numbers of homicides elsewhere in L.A. appear to offer some evidence for the effectiveness of the initiative. Following the intervention, the total number of violent crimes, gang crimes, and gun crimes also decreased in Hollenbeck (Table 3.1). For the three comparison areas, we compared changes in crime for three periods of time: the six months prior to the event—the *pre-intervention* period; the four months in which all elements of the intervention were applied at one time or another—the *suppression* period; and the two months in which only selected parts of the intervention, such as heightened patrol of public housing units in the area and greater enforcement of probation and parole regulations, were

Table 3.1

Crime Trends in Hollenbeck

	Number of crimes in the six months . . .		
	. . . before intervention	. . . after intervention	Change
Violent crimes	918	663	−28%
Gang crimes	259	177	−32%
Gun crimes	490	330	−33%

consistently applied—the *deterrence* period (Table 3.2). A reduction in crime in the treatment areas greater than those in the comparison areas during the suppression period would help show the effects of all measures combined, whereas continuing reductions in the deter-

Table 3.2

Intervention Activities by Month

	Period					
	Suppression				Deterrence	
Intervention Tactic	1	2	3	4	5	6
Saturation patrol (Metro)	+	+				
Central Bureau SEU gang enforcement	+	+	+	+		
Housing police patrols	+	+	+	+	+	+
Probation, parole and warrant searches	8	8	8	7	+	+
Probation, parole, and warrant arrests	4	3	1	1		
Referrals for federal gun prosecutions		3	1			
Nuisance property abate-ment	+					
Traffic control and other barriers	+					
Retailing the message	+	+	+			

NOTE: + indicates activity above baseline level that is not quantified. Numbers indicate counts of actions occurring during the time period.

rence period would suggest that the intervention may have had some long-term effects in changing behavior, or that short-term application of some resources can produce a long-term deterrence effect (although we recognize our measure of deterrence is confounded by the continuation of some suppression activities).

METHODOLOGY

We observed the counts of all violent crimes, gun crimes, and gang crimes in the treatment (or intervention) site and the control (or comparison) sites. We assumed that the observed counts in the control site have a Poisson distribution with mean λ_t. There is a different mean for each of the 12 study months, including the six months prior to the intervention, the four months of the suppression period, and the two months of the deterrence period.

In the absence of any intervention, we assumed that the average number of events in the treatment site is a fixed fraction, k_1, of the average number in the control site. (We assess the plausibility of this assumption after presenting our results.) Under our proportionality assumption, the number of events in each of the pre-intervention months has mean $k_1 \times \lambda_t$ for the intervention sites. When the suppression phase began in month 7 we assumed that the average number of events in the intervention site changed to $k_2 \times \lambda_t$, for $t = 7, 8, 9,$ 10. These four months correspond with the suppression period. Last, the average number of events in each of the months in the intervention site might change yet again after the intervention period ended, to $k_3 \times \lambda_t$ for $t = 11, 12$. This is the deterrence period that corresponds with the diminished level of direct intervention activity. Each k represents the ratio of the expected number of events in the intervention site to the expected number of events in the control site. Table 3.3 shows an example for all violent events in the five RDs versus the rest of Boyle Heights. The fifth and sixth columns show the assumed average number of events for each month by site.

If the control area is well matched to the treatment area, then in the absence of an intervention we would expect the rate of incidents in the treatment area to be $k_1 \times \lambda_t$ throughout the study period. Therefore, the suppression effect, $k_2 - k_1$, and the deterrence effect, $k_3 - k_1$,

Table 3.3

Example of Data Structure

	Month	Events in Five Targeted RDs (Treatment Area)	Events in Remainder of Boyle Heights (Control Area)	Average Number of Events in Control Area	Average Number of Events in Treatment Area
Pre-intervention	1	21	81	λ_1	$k_1 \times \lambda_1$
	2	25	57	λ_2	$k_1 \times \lambda_2$
	3	28	62	λ_3	$k_1 \times \lambda_3$
	4	21	86	l_4	$k_1 \times \lambda_4$
	5	24	68	λ_5	$k_1 \times \lambda_5$
	6	29	46	λ_6	$k_1 \times \lambda_6$
Suppression	7	22	56	λ_7	$k_2 \times \lambda_7$
	8	9	59	λ_8	$k_2 \times \lambda_8$
	9	14	55	λ_9	$k_2 \times \lambda_9$
	10	21	50	λ_{10}	$k_2 \times \lambda_{10}$
Deterrence	11	11	35	λ_{11}	$k_3 \times \lambda_{11}$
	12	15	58	λ_{12}	$k_3 \times \lambda_{12}$

measure the degree to which the observed crime trends differ from what we would have observed if the intervention was withheld. From estimates of $\lambda_1, \ldots, \lambda_{12}$ and of k_1, k_2, k_3 we estimated the suppression effect and the deterrence effect.

The λ_t's are not completely unrelated quantities. The average in month 2 is likely to be similar to the average in month 1. Therefore we modeled the $\log(\lambda_t)$ as an autoregressive process,

$$\log \lambda_t = \mu + \varepsilon_t, \quad \varepsilon_t \sim N(\theta \varepsilon_{t-1}, \tau^2)$$

Special cases of this model include an independent error model (when $\theta = 0$) and a constant rate model (when $\theta = 0$ and $\tau^2 = 0$). However, we estimated both θ and τ^2 jointly with the other model parameters. Conditional on a fixed λ_t, the observed counts are assumed to have a Poisson distribution, but in practice the observed variation in count outcomes is often greater than what would be expected under the Poisson distribution That is the so-called extra-Poisson variation or overdispersion. The autoregressive model on $\log (\lambda_t)$ propagates additional variation to the marginal distribution of the observed counts, mitigating potential problems with over-dispersion.

Our results tables show Bayes estimators computed for each comparison by each crime type. The tables show the mean and standard deviation of the suppression and deterrence effects. We also computed the probability that k_1 is less than k_2 and the probability that k_1 is less than k_3. These probabilities indicate the probability that the intervention was *ineffective,* and therefore small probabilities indicate intervention effectiveness.

EFFECTS IN BOYLE HEIGHTS AND THE REMAINDER OF HOLLENBECK

What broad effects might the intervention have had in Boyle Heights—all of which received "retailing" of the intervention message and some increased social services—that were not evident in the remainder of Hollenbeck? Following the intervention, gang and gun crime decreased more rapidly in Boyle Heights than in the remainder of Hollenbeck, effects that may be attributable to the intervention, whereas violent crime decreased at similar rates in both Boyle Heights and in the remainder of Hollenbeck.

Violent Crime

There was more crime in Boyle Heights than in the remainder of Hollenbeck in both the six months of the pre-intervention periods and the combined six months of the suppression and deterrence periods. In the six-month pre-intervention period, there were 546 violent crimes in Boyle Heights and 372 in the remainder of Hollenbeck. During the six-month intervention period, violent crime decreased by nearly identical rates in both areas, or by about 28 percent in both areas. The number of violent crimes in both areas following the intervention was also similar.

In a comparison of the effects of the intervention by period, there appears to have been no greater reduction of crime in Boyle Heights than in the remainder of Hollenbeck during the suppression period, whereas violent crime in the two months of the deterrence period decreased more rapidly in Boyle Heights than it did in the remainder of Hollenbeck (Table 3.4). Our analysis showed that, given the observed trends in violent crimes, the probability that the Boyle Heights violent crime rate was greater during the suppression period than what it would have been without the intervention is 63 percent. While a 63 percent probability indicates little evidence of any change in violent crime rates during the suppression phase, the violent crime trends showed substantial evidence of a decrease in violent crime rates relative to what we would have expected during the deterrence phase in the absence of an intervention. Because we have no theoretical explanation why "retailing" the intervention message and offering social services prior to the intervention would have an effect several months later, we consider the finding of an effect in the deterrence period to be an artifact of the model rather than a reflection of true deterrence.

Gang Crime

The broadest elements of the intervention appear to be associated with greater reductions in gang crime in Boyle Heights than in the remainder of Hollenbeck. The probability of an ineffective treatment during the suppression phase was 4.7 percent and during the deter-

Table 3.4

Comparative Change in Violent Crime in Boyle Heights and the Remainder of Hollenbeck

		Mean	SD	95% CI
	Treatment Rate Multiplier			
	k_1	1.516	0.1049	1.320–1.732
	k_2	1.583	0.1519	1.309–1.902
	k_3	1.158	0.1441	0.902–1.461
	Treatment Effect			
Suppression	$(k_2 - k_1)$	0.0668	0.1881	
	$P(k_1 < k_2) = 0.63$			
Deterrence	$(k_3 - k_1)$	−0.3581	0.1742	
	$P(k_1 < k_3) = 0.024$			

Table 3.5

**Comparative Change in Gang Crime in Boyle Heights
and the Remainder of Hollenbeck**

		Mean	SD	95% CI
		Treatment Rate Multiplier		
	k_1	0.9902	0.1261	0.7643–1.2570
	k_2	0.7022	0.1242	0.4909–0.9775
	k_3	0.5578	0.1345	0.3292–0.8551
		Treatment Effect		
Suppression	$(k_2 - k_1)$	−0.288	0.1712	
	$P(k_1 < k_2) = 0.047$			
Deterrence	$(k_3 - k_1)$	−0.4324	0.1803	
	$P(k_1 < k_3) = 0.009$			

rence phase was even lower at 0.9 percent (Table 3.5). The difference in the rate of gang crime was statistically significant in both periods and even stronger in the deterrence period than in the prior suppression period. This suggests that the broadest elements of the intervention may have had a discernible effect on both suppressing gang crime and deterring some gang criminal behavior.

Gun Crime

The reductions for gun crime paralleled those for gang crime. The rate of gun crime decreased in Boyle Heights relative to the remainder of Hollenbeck during the intervention period and further decreased in the deterrence period (Table 3.6). In other words, the reduction in gun crime throughout Boyle Heights may have been associated with the intervention that began during the suppression period and continued during the deterrence period.

EFFECTS IN THE TARGETED REPORTING DISTRICTS AND THE REMAINDER OF BOYLE HEIGHTS

What effects did the law enforcement portions of the intervention (e.g., increased patrols, enforcement of parole and probation condi-

Table 3.6

Comparative Change in Gun Crime in Boyle Heights
and the Remainder of Hollenbeck

		Mean	SD	95% CI
	Treatment Rate Multiplier			
	k_1	0.3814	0.037	0.3136–0.4588
	k_2	0.2994	0.0405	0.2287–0.3876
	k_3	0.2555	0.0556	0.1599–0.3777
	Treatment Effect			
Suppression	$(k_2 - k_1)$ −0.82	0.0541		
	$P(k_1 < k_2) =$ 0.066			
Deterrence	$(k_3 - k_1)$ −0.126	0.0672		
	$P(k_1 < k_3) =$ 0.039			

tions) have in the targeted reporting districts that were not evident in the remainder of Boyle Heights? The intervention appears to have been associated with a reduction in violent crime and gang crime in the targeted RDs, but any effects it had on gun crime were not statistically significant.

Violent Crime

In the six months prior to the triggering event, there were 148 violent crimes in the five RDs receiving the full intervention and 400 such incidents in the remainder of Boyle Heights. In the six months subsequent to the intervention, violent crime in the targeted RDs decreased 37 percent to 92, but only 24 percent in the remainder of Boyle Heights, to 303.

The difference in rate of decrease between the targeted RDs and the remainder of Boyle Heights was statistically significant in both periods and even stronger in the deterrence period than in the suppression period (Table 3.7). This suggests that the full law enforcement intervention may have had a discernible effect on both suppressing gang crime and deterring some gang criminal behavior in the targeted RDs.

Table 3.7

Comparative Change in Violent Crime in Targeted RDs and Remainder of Boyle Heights

	Mean	SD	95% CI
Treatment Rate Multiplier			
k_1 1.673	0.1533		1.384–1.988
k_2 1.335	0.1506		1.067–1.655
k_3 1.163	0.1909		0.8314–1.578
Treatment Effect			
Suppression $(k_2 - k_1)$ –0.3381	0.1968		
$P(k_1 < k_2) = 0.047$			
Deterrence $(k_3 - k_1)$ –0.5093	0.2368		
$P(k_1 < k_3) = 0.024$			

Gang Crime

In the six months prior to the triggering event, there were 36 gang crimes in the targeted RDs and 139 such crimes in the remainder of Boyle Heights. In the subsequent six months, there were 29 gang crimes in the targeted RDs, a decrease of 19 percent, and 76 such crimes in the remainder of Hollenbeck, a decrease of 45 percent. Although the rate of decrease for the entire six-month period was greater in the remainder of Boyle Heights than in the targeted RDs, our statistical analysis shows that the decrease in gang crime during the four months of the suppression period in the targeted RDs was greater than the decrease in the remainder of Boyle Heights (Table 3.8).

Gun Crime

During the intervention, gun crime fell at nearly identical rates in the target area (33 percent) and the remainder of Boyle Heights (32 percent). There was no statistical evidence of a difference between these trends (Table 3.9). The small number of gun crimes in the area—

Table 3.8

Comparative Change in Gang Crime in Targeted RDs and Remainder of Boyle Heights

		Mean	SD	95% CI
Treatment Rate Multiplier				
	k_1	0.9293	0.1609	0.6413–1.272
	k_2	0.5729	0.1439	0.3391–0.9005
	k_3	0.9552	0.2685	0.5311–1.567
Treatment Effect				
Suppression	$(k_2 - k_1)$	−0.3585	0.2004	
	$P(k_1 < k_2) = 0.038$			
Deterrence	$(k_3 - k_1)$	−0.5082	0.3007	
	$P(k_1 < k_3) = 0.508$			

Table 3.9

Comparative Change in Gun Crime in Targeted RDs and Remainder of Boyle Heights

		Mean	SD	95% CI
Treatment Rate Multiplier				
	k_1	0.3491	0.0492	0.2623–0.4545
	k_2	0.2831	0.0564	0.1888–0.4090
	k_3	0.4143	0.1072	0.2365–0.6536
Treatment Effect				
Suppression	$(k_2 - k_1)$	−0.0661	0.0745	
	$P(k_1 < k_2) = 0.185$			
Deterrence	$(k_3 - k_1)$	0.0652	0.1212	
	$P(k_1 < k_3) = 0.688$			

about ten per month for the targeted RDs—may be a reason why no change in gun crime seems to be associated with the intervention in our statistical analysis.

EFFECTS IN THE TARGETED REPORTING DISTRICTS AND A MATCHED GROUP OF HOLLENBECK CENSUS BLOCK GROUPS

Because Boyle Heights is more heterogeneous than the targeted RDs, we sought to compare changes in crime following the intervention in the targeted area with a more closely matched comparable area. More specifically, we analyzed Census block statistics for the area comprising the targeted RDs and identified comparable Census block groups within Hollenbeck for comparison (Figure 3.1).

Reporting districts are nearly coterminous with Census tracts. Each RD therefore comprises Census block groups just as each Census tract does. Census block groups are preferable to RDs or Census tracts for this analysis, however, because they allow analysis of the true target areas, or of areas most closely matching the turf of targeted gangs.

Our matching method involved specifying a probability model (logit or probit) and computing predicted values of a block group being selected for intervention. The estimated probability of a block group being selected for the intervention is the propensity score (Rosenbaum and Rubin, 1983, 1984), or the predicted probability that a particular place, given its characteristics, will adopt a particular program (Bartik, 2002). This method has been used to evaluate enterprise zones for economic development (Greenbaum and Engberg, 1998; Engberg and Greenbaum, 1999; Bondonio and Engberg, 2000), job training programs (Dehejia and Wahba, 1999), and how violence affects local business decisions (Greenbaum and Tita, 2002).

The only apparent use of such a technique within the criminal justice literature is by Grogger (2002) in his analysis of the efficacy of civil injunctions against gangs in Los Angeles County. His method differs from ours in that he matched areas solely on their levels of crime. We controlled for both levels of crime and the structural variables (e.g., income, poverty, residential stability, population density, educational attainment, and age structure) thought to influence levels of crime. According to criminological theory, places with similar at-

Figure 3.1—Intervention and Control Area Census Block Groups

tributes should experience similar levels of crime and similar changes in these levels over time. Greenbaum and Tita (2002) demonstrated the utility of this approach in examining how "surges" in local levels of violence affected local business activity. As Greenbaum and Tita did, we first estimated a probit model where the dependent variable is coded "1" if a Census block group receives the intervention and "0" if it does not. The independent measures in the model included the number of violent and gang-related crimes in the pre-intervention period, per capita income, percentage in poverty, percentage of occupied housing units that are rented, percentage of population that moved into current residence within the five years prior to the Census, population density, percentage of population at least 18 years of age that has not graduated high school, and percentage of population 15 to 24 years of age.

The purpose of modeling the outcome variable as a function of these particular covariates is to gain the most precise matched sample rather than to conduct hypothesis testing of theoretical questions. We therefore used stepwise (forward loading) regression to choose among the list of covariates that provide the most robust estimated probabilities, or propensity scores. We used STATA statistical software (v. 7.0) to estimate the model. After we specified a model containing all of the above covariates, our stepwise estimation process yielded five variables—income, poverty, households that rent, population density, and population mobility—that were useful in predicting which Census block groups in Boyle Heights were most similar to those included in the intervention. We used the estimates produced from this model (and the STATA "predict" command) to predict propensity scores for all Census block groups in Hollenbeck so as to identify the best matches with the intervention neighborhood throughout the area. The resulting propensity scores for targeted and matched block groups are shown in Table 3.10 (see Figure 3.1 for a map of the block groups).

Comparing the Census block groups of the targeted areas with those of matched block groups (the control areas), we see greater reductions in violent crime, but not in gang or gun crime, in the targeted area than in the control area.

Violent Crime

In the six months following the intervention, the number of violent crimes in the targeted Census block groups decreased 34 percent, while those in the matched Census block groups decreased only 3

Table 3.10

Propensity Score Matches

Treatment Block Group ID	Propensity Score	Propensity Score of Match	Matched Block Group ID
204403	0.243	0.247	203403
204601	0.347	0.351	205104
204505	0.601	0.584	199901
204504	0.736	0.766	201704
204506	0.835	0.861	203403
204503	0.903	0.890	203102

percent. The intervention effect seemed to be greatest in the suppression period and diminished slightly in the deterrence period (Table 3.11). This suggests there may have been a reduction in crime associated with the intervention in the targeted block groups that began in the suppression period and continued for at least part of the deterrence period.

Table 3.11

Comparative Change in Violent Crime in Targeted and Matched Census Block Groups

		Mean	SD	95% CI
	Treatment Rate Multiplier			
	k_1	2.351	0.3209	1.794–3.033
	k_2	1.595	0.3183	1.089–2.332
	k_3	1.698	0.3826	1.056–2.554
	Treatment Effect			
Suppression	$(k_2 - k_1)$	−0.7558	0.4327	
	$P(k_1 < k_2) = 0.048$			
Deterrence	$(k_3 - k_1)$	−0.653	0.4668	
	$P(k_1 < k_3) = 0.082$			

Gang Crime

The intervention does not appear to have had any significant effect on gang crime in the targeted Census block groups in comparison with the matched block groups (Table 3.12). There are several possible explanations for this lack of effect.

First, there are a relatively small number of gang crimes in the targeted and matched areas; in the targeted area, there were 30 such crimes in the six months before the intervention and 28 such crimes in the six months afterward, while in the matched area there were 23 gang crimes in each period. It is possible that the generally low number of such crimes makes it difficult to test the effects the intervention might have had.

Second, "lesser" gangs (as measured in number of members, number of rivalries, or length of history) can often have erratic patterns in their violence and be unable to sustain their peak levels of violence because of attrition. If, for example, a particularly violent or charismatic member is in some way incapacitated (either by jail or by a bullet), a gang can virtually cease to exist.

Table 3.12

Comparative Change in Gang Crime in Targeted and Matched Census Block Groups

		Mean	SD	95% CI
	Treatment Rate Multiplier			
	k_1	0.8171	0.2047	0.4757–1.268
	k_2	0.518	0.1805	0.2326–0.9342
	k_3	1.376	0.4585	0.662–2.435
	Treatment Effect			
Suppression	$(k_2 - k_1)$	−0.299	0.2507	
	$P(k_1 < k_2) = 0.108$			
Deterrence	$(k_3 - k_1)$	0.5585	0.4770	
	$P(k_1 < k_3) = 0.901$			

Third, our matching process may not have accounted for potentially unique aspects of TMC and Cuatro Flats. Many working group members identified these gangs as the most problematic; therefore, they may be the most difficult to control.

Gun Crime

In the six months before the intervention, there were 53 gun crimes in the treatment area and 62 in the control area. In the six months following the intervention, there were 38 such crimes in the treatment area and 51 in the control area. While the decrease in the treatment area (28 percent) was greater than that in the control area (18 percent), in neither the suppression nor the deterrence period was the difference between the areas statistically significant (Table 3.13). Again, it is possible that the generally low number of such crimes makes it difficult to test the effects the intervention might have had.

Table 3.13

Comparative Change in Gun Crime in Targeted and Matched Census Block Groups

		Mean	SD	95% CI
	Treatment Rate Multiplier			
	k_1	0.3145	0.06	0.2093–0.4446
	k_2	0.221	0.0786	0.1010–0.4052
	k_3	0.6197	0.1974	0.3138–1.083
	Treatment Effect			
Suppression	$(k_2 - k_1)$	−0.0935	0.1009	
	$P(k_1 < k_2) = 0.167$			
Deterrence	$(k_3 - k_1)$	0.3052	0.2064	
	$P(k_1 < k_3) = 0.958$			

ASSESSING MODEL ASSUMPTIONS

The above analyses depend on the assumption that the average number of incidents in the intervention area is proportional to the average number in the comparison areas—or that seasonal changes, alterations in law enforcement, and other variables influencing violent crime affect the intervention and comparison areas equally, with differences in number of events due only to changes in the size of the site, the number of residents, and the number of individuals with a propensity to commit violent offenses. We consider this assumption plausible because both sites receive the same basic policing and social services.

To test this assumption further, we examined the number of incidents in the 11 months preceding the intervention. For each month, we estimated the ratio of the average number of events in the intervention area to the number in the comparison area. If these estimated ratios are roughly constant then we can conclude that the proportionality assumption is reasonable.

Figure 3.2 shows the ratio of the number of crimes in the intervention area to the number in each of the three comparison areas for each of the three types of crime we analyzed. Each row shows a different type of crime, while each column shows comparisons between different areas. For example, the top left cell shows the ratio of gun crimes (top row) in the targeted Census block groups to those in the matched sample blocks (left column), while the middle cell shows the ratio of gang crimes (middle row) in Boyle Heights (BH) to the remainder of Hollenbeck (RH) (middle column), and the bottom right cell shows the ratio of violent crimes (bottom row) in the targeted RDs to the remainder of Boyle Heights (right column).

In nearly every circumstance, we found that the average ratio (shown by the horizontal line in each cell) was within a 95 percent prediction band, as indicated by the shaded areas. In several cells, there is a great degree of variability in the ratios, a result of small sample sizes (or numbers of observed crimes), but the overall evidence indicates that the proportionality assumption on which our methodology rests is valid.

OTHER ANALYSES

Although the intervention—and hence our formal statistical analyses—was targeted at a specific area and the gangs that inhabit it, we might expect it to affect neighboring areas and gangs. Accordingly,

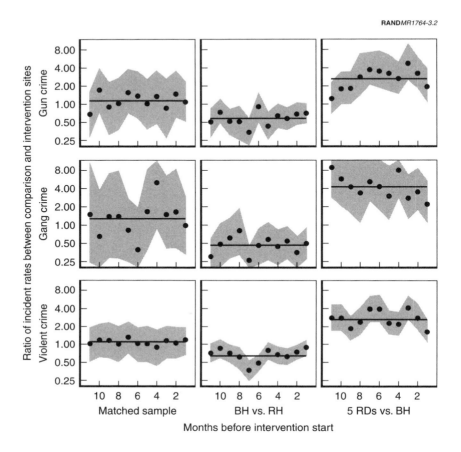

Figure 3.2—Crime Ratios in Comparison Areas

we review briefly some evidence of effects of the intervention on surrounding areas and their gangs.

Past analyses of locally focused policing interventions (Clarke, 1992; Grogger, 2002; Barr and Pease, 1990) have found that the benefits of such initiatives often disperse to wider areas. That is, when a locally focused policing intervention reduces crime in the target area, crime also falls in immediately adjacent areas.

We found a similar dispersion of benefits in the Hollenbeck project. Reductions in crime in the targeted Census block groups were matched or exceeded by those in the 11 surrounding block groups (Table 3.14).

Because the initiative focused on gang crime and was triggered by an incident involving two specific gangs, we analyzed the effects of the initiative on particular gangs in two ways. First, we reviewed the number of incidents involving members of TMC and Cuatro Flats, the two gangs involved in the triggering incident. Second, we examined how the initiative may have affected other specific gangs.

Using LAPD gang incident data, we found that, within the Hollenbeck area, there were 30 incidents involving a TMC or Cuatro Flats gang member (either offender or victim) in the six months prior to the intervention and 26 such incidents in the six months after the intervention (Figure 3.3). While the total number of incidents in the two periods is not significantly different, the month-to-month trend does suggest a significant effect of the initiative during the suppression period. The monthly number of incidents involving these two

Table 3.14

Crime in Targeted and Surrounding Census Block Groups

	Block groups	
	Targeted 6	Surrounding 11
Violent crime in the six months . . .		
. . . before intervention	109	93
. . . after intervention	72	62
Percent reduction	*−34%*	*−33%*
Gang crime in the six months . . .		
. . . before intervention	53	50
. . . after intervention	38	28
Percent reduction	*−28%*	*−44%*
Gun crime in the six months . . .		
. . . before intervention	23	18
. . . after intervention	17	13
Percent reduction	*−26%*	*−28%*

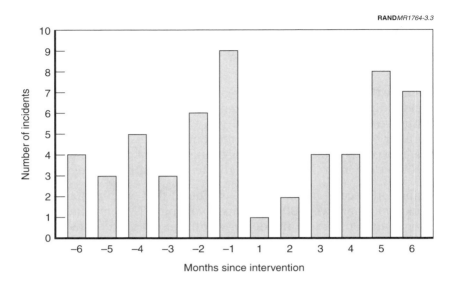

RAND*MR1764-3.3*

Months since intervention

Figure 3.3—Hollenbeck Area Crimes Involving TMC or Cuatro Flats Gang Members Before and After Operation Ceasefire

gangs increased sharply before the intervention and did not return to pre-intervention levels until five months after the intervention.

It is possible, of course, that TMC and Cuatro Flats gang members shifted their activity to different areas. We do not believe this is the case, however, given the parochial nature of street gangs and the fact that members of the Hollenbeck initiative working group who were sharing intelligence with law enforcement officials in other areas did not report any increases in activity by these gangs elsewhere.

It is also possible that focusing on particular gangs may affect the activity of other gangs. If a particular gang is facing additional attention and patrol by the police, its rivals may use this opportunity to increase their activity because policing is likely to have diminished in its own area. Alternatively, police suppression of criminal activity by members of a gang may similarly suppress criminal activity by its rivals, at least to the extent of spatial concentration of interactions among gangs.

Other than Cuatro Flats, the only other identified rival for TMC (as shown in Figure 2.1) is Primera Flats, an ally of Cuatro Flats. In the six months prior to the incident between TMC and Cuatro Flats that triggered the intervention, there were ten incidents involving Primera Flats members, in eight of which they were offenders. In the six months following the start of the intervention, there were only six incidents, in two of which Primera Flats members were offenders.

Cuatro Flats has many rivalries among gangs in south Hollenbeck (or that portion of the area south of the San Bernardino Freeway), including, in addition to TMC, Breed Street, Clarence Street, East LA Dukes, and KAM (Hazard, its remaining rival, is north of the freeway). In the six months prior to the intervention, these four gangs were involved in 65 incidents, in 43 of which they were offenders. In the six months following the intervention, they were involved in 23 incidents, in 12 of which they were offenders.

While we cannot directly attribute decreasing crime by these gangs to the intervention against TMC and Cuatro Flats, it is intriguing that both the targeted gangs and their rivals decreased their criminal activity following the intervention. This is true in part because Cuatro Flats and TMC members decreased their victimization of these gangs from eight incidents in the six months prior to the intervention to two afterward. These results suggest that focused law enforcement against two gangs helped quell the activities of their rivals.

The focus of the intervention on two gangs and their turf also affected the turf or areas in which their rivals were concentrated. Each rival gang of the targeted gangs is known to occupy a specific geographic area within Hollenbeck. One can therefore combine the social network information with the spatial distribution of gang turf to compute a set of control areas that are "socially tied" to the targeted areas. A "social lag model" based on such social and geographic information may explain the distribution of crime and the benefits of an intervention against it better than a "spatial lag model" based solely on geographic proximity (Tita, 2002).

In the areas of rival gangs socially tied to the targeted gangs (see Figure 3.4), there were 35 gang crimes involving guns (the specific kind of problem that launched the intervention) prior to the intervention; in the six months following the intervention, the number of such crimes decreased to 26, a 26 percent drop. This matched in magnitude the 26 percent decrease in such crimes in the areas of the targeted gangs, from 23 in the six months prior to the intervention to 17 in the six months afterward. In other words, the intervention appears to have helped reduce gang crimes involving guns both in the turf of the targeted gangs and in the turf of their rivals.

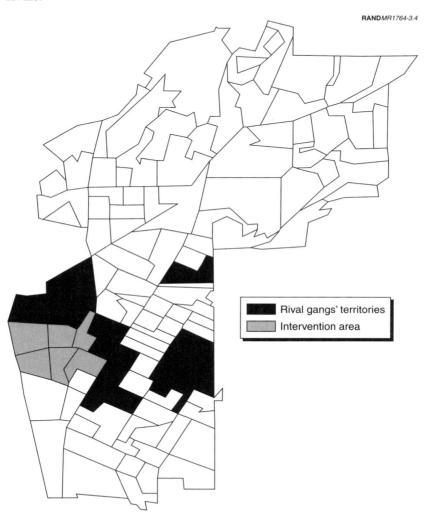

RAND*MR1764-3.4*

Rival gangs' territories

Intervention area

Figure 3.4—Map of TMC and Cuatro Flats Territory (Intervention Area) and Rival Gangs' Territories

Chapter Four

IMPLICATIONS FOR FUTURE ADAPTATIONS

What do the results of Operation Ceasefire in Hollenbeck indicate for future adaptations of similar initiatives? To answer this question, we review the effects of the Hollenbeck initiative. We also look at how well the initiative was implemented and how similar initiatives might be implemented more easily and effectively.

OVERALL EFFECTS OF THE INITIATIVE

The broadest parts of the initiative, particularly "retailing" the message of the pending implementation in the hope that the news would lead to widespread reduction of crime in the wake of actual implementation, appears to have had no discernible effect on crime in the immediate aftermath of implementation or during the suppression period. We could only measure the value of the broad parts of the initiative in correspondingly broad areas (or for Boyle Heights and the remainder of Hollenbeck), and it is possible that these components had an effect that we could not analyze in smaller areas. Nevertheless, such an effect seems unlikely, in part because, given the way in which the broadest parts of the initiative were implemented, there is no logical reason for their effects to be concentrated in a smaller area. It is more likely that the broadest elements of the initiative are simply too weak a lever to affect violent, gang, or gun crime.

In contrast, the law enforcement components of the intervention showed more promising effects. In four of the six comparisons in our formal statistical analysis of violent crime and gang crime, we found reductions of crime in the targeted areas during the suppression period to be significantly greater than in the comparison areas. In none of the three comparisons in our formal statistical analysis of gun crime did we fine statistically significant differences, although in our broadest pair of comparison areas (Boyle Heights with the remainder of Hollenbeck), we found a difference in gun crime that approached statistical significance in the suppression period and that was statistically significant in the deterrence period, suggesting an effect against gun crime that began sometime in the suppression period and continued into the deterrence period.

Other analyses also suggest that the effects of the intervention decreased over time. In analyzing behavior by the targeted gangs, for example, we found a sharp decrease in violent offending for the first four months of the intervention, or during the suppression period, but increases to pre-intervention levels in the fifth and sixth months, or during the deterrence period.

Nevertheless, in our statistical analyses across various levels of geographically defined comparison groups, we found reductions during the deterrence period of violent crime, gang crime, and gun crime that were greater in Boyle Heights than in Hollenbeck and of violent crime that was greater in the targeted reporting districts than in the remainder of Boyle Heights.

In addition, while none of the differences during the deterrence period between the targeted and matched Census block groups was statistically significant, we found that the difference in violent crime between these small areas during this period approached statistical significance. Coupled with the statistically significant difference in the suppression period, this finding suggests that at least some of the effect of retailing the message persisted into the deterrence period.

Our ability to measure a "pure" deterrence effect was limited by the fact that some suppression activities persisted into the deterrence period. If the deterrence effects we detected are attributable to these continuing suppression activities, then it is possible that the deterrence activities of the intervention may by themselves be insufficient, in the absence of additional law enforcement measures, to abate crime.

More disappointing was our inability to test the value of a dynamic intervention. Without the dynamic component of the program, we cannot determine whether the program could have suppressed or deterred crime in all of Boyle Heights, how long the intervention would have had to have been sustained to achieve such an effect, or whether a true deterrent effect could have been achieved.

WHAT WORKED

Perhaps the most important success of the program was the success of the working group—using data analysis and with collaboration from many different agencies—in achieving a well-designed intervention. One working group participant from the LAPD noted, "No one ever thought this was a bad idea. In fact, it makes sense. But departmental resources were never made available to implement the model in the intended way." Through the working group process, individual organizations were able to design a collaborative intervention and contribute resources sufficient for the initiative.

We learned it is possible for diverse criminal justice organizations, including police, prosecutors, and probation officers, to work together effectively. The experience confirmed what members had supposed: Each organization had unique resources that, when pooled with those of the others, made it more effective in curbing violence than it could have been alone. While a single probation officer, no matter how dedicated, may not have much effect in reducing crime, that officer's ability to use information from other agencies in a timely manner could multiply whatever effect the officer might have.

The working group itself provided a regular forum for individuals to exchange ideas and, perhaps more important, a forum for focusing attention on a discrete and manageable problem. It also helped develop community support for the collaboration that exceeded our expectations. Tailoring the intervention against an activity, such as gun violence, rather than an affiliation, such as gang membership, helped make it possible for the community to support the intervention. Community support helped the working group enlist a county supervisor in securing grants from the county probation department for hiring an intervention specialist to support the project.

Community support also led the city attorney's office to dedicate both a prosecutor and community organizer to the project. The prosecutor was instrumental in taking actions regarding code violations at properties where gang members congregated, while the community organizer helped bring together both those providing law enforcement components of the intervention and those who would have provided social services.

WHAT COULD HAVE WORKED BETTER

As noted in Chapter Two, the program was not implemented as originally conceived, in that it never included a process for dynamic responses. One reason this capability was never implemented was the reorganization, about six months before the intervention was launched, of LAPD gang units in the wake of the Rampart scandal in which several Rampart gang unit members were accused of planting evidence and excessive use of force. The disbanding of all previously existing gang units meant that many knowledgeable officers who would have participated in the project were no longer available to it. It was also difficult for new gang unit officers to become familiar with the more than 30 gangs operating in the area. The new gang unit staff was quickly able to focus its attention on the most problematic gangs in Hollenbeck, including TMC and Cuatro Flats, but it was not able to quickly acquire the detailed knowledge needed for a more dynamic intervention concerning the vulnerabilities of members in other gangs.

While the community supported the working group and its processes in designing and implementing an intervention, the working group members never truly assumed "ownership" of the project. One objective of the project had been to create a standing mechanism through which members of the working group could continually address problems of violence in the community. Although it was important for the project to be driven by research, it was also important for working group members to develop a collaboration that could evolve beyond the sponsorship of the original research partner. We did not succeed in developing such self-supporting collaboration, or in transferring "ownership" of the project from RAND to the working group. Many working group members continually referred to the project as the "RAND study" or the "RAND project." These statements by the working group members indicate a sense that in their minds the changes we sought were needed only for the period of the initial study and not for continuing interagency and community collaboration and operating procedures.

One reason for this failure to develop a self-sustaining process was the frequent rotation of agency personnel with whom the working group collaborated. During the 18 months of the most intensive planning, for example, researchers interacted with a half dozen LAPD captains. While such turnover may have been inevitable given the larger organizational changes within the LAPD at that time, the fact remains that it did not foster the stability needed to help the project sustain itself beyond the period of support provided by RAND.

Another reason the working group process did not become self-sustaining was the lack of resources for any single agency to manage and maintain the collaboration. Agency budgets are not structured to encourage cross-agency collaboration, nor are agency personnel evaluated for their participation in such efforts. For such efforts to succeed, city governments—in L.A. or elsewhere—must find mechanisms to encourage these interagency exercises, either through appropriations or through other processes.

Changes in the political leadership of the city, especially within the District Attorney's office and the U.S. Attorney's office following the November 2000 elections, also presented some obstacles to implementing and sustaining the initiative. While the interim U.S. Attorney supported our efforts and pledged to prosecute federal gun crimes referred by the project, the contact person for the project changed frequently. Because only federal agents can actually file federal cases, and neither the F.B.I. nor the Bureau of Alcohol, Tobacco, and Firearms had a designated contact for the initiative, referring gun cases for federal prosecution was a cumbersome process. The U.S. Attorney's office and the F.B.I. did agree to make two LAPD detectives eligible to file cases resulting from the project, but the cross-designation was never completed.

While the District Attorney's office was an enthusiastic supporter of prosecuting at all levels gun crimes reported by the initiative, the new prosecutorial administration that took office after the November 2000 election cooled on the idea. Instead of being handled by a specific contact person within the District Attorney's office, Operation Ceasefire cases were treated no differently from any other case referred for prosecution. Many cases from the project therefore resulted in plea bargains, an outcome that undermined the ability of the initiative to increase the certainty and severity of punishment for gun-related offenses.

The inability of the project to attract personnel from participating agencies who were designated specifically and exclusively for the project was frustrating but not unexpected. Except for the research partner, Operation Ceasefire did not provide funds to any participating organization. Participating-agency personnel had to maintain their regular duties outside the project. Even project staff from the LAPD and the county probation office, the two organizations that dedicated the most time to the project, had to maintain their regular responsibilities elsewhere.

Without personnel able to devote time exclusively to the initiative, the project lacked accountability for its success or failure. Because participants were not evaluated based on their performance on the project and therefore did not see it as their primary responsibility, some were more worried about deflecting blame should the initiative fail. Even project failure was seen not as something that would affect individual careers but as something that might make an organization look bad among its peers.

RECOMMENDATIONS

To execute interagency initiatives such as Operation Ceasefire, agencies—particularly those in an area as large as Los Angeles—need to focus on developing concrete mechanisms to support collaboration. The components of the criminal justice system do not typically work together in a way to bring the resources of all to bear on specific problems such as that presented by Hollenbeck gang violence. In short, there is a need to make the criminal justice "system" more systematic.

City leaders likewise need to consider establishing processes to support agencies in such collaborations and to hold them accountable. Most agencies have limited flexibility in their budgets, and almost none have the ability to redirect resources for such collaborations. Few agency directors are evaluated on how well they collaborate with other agencies. To build future collaboration, city leaders should ensure that support and accountability measures are considered in future budgets and evaluations.

To support future collaborations, cost information on such projects is needed. One reason there are so few interagency collaborations such as Operation Ceasefire is that such efforts are considered cumbersome and expensive. Most evaluations (including this one) of interagency collaborations to reduce crime have focused almost exclusively on how much crime actually decreased. Calculating the true costs in staff time and overhead expenses for such projects is necessary for determining whether such interventions merit replication or continuation.

More generally, those who adapt initiatives like the Boston project to areas like Hollenbeck or elsewhere must recognize that the violence each community confronts has unique features and that providing prevention and social intervention programs can be an especially difficult task. As we noted previously, adapting the principles of the Boston project to Hollenbeck required adapting from a citywide to a neighborhood initiative; from an initiative targeted to African American youth to one targeted to intergenerational Latino gangs; from one with resources in place for a dynamic intervention to one with fewer resources—because, in response to two problematic gangs, community leaders believed implementation was necessary before all planning was completed. Merely adapting the initiative to other Los Angeles communities would require attention to issues leading to still further modification. Representatives of other Angeleno neighborhoods, for example, including treatment providers and case workers, report that, unlike Hollenbeck, where gang violence stems from inter-gang rivalries, gang problems elsewhere stem from intra-gang rivalries, especially when former gang leaders returning to their community from prison seek to reassume their former roles and leadership in the gang.

Such local assumptions should be subjected to research before any intervention is undertaken. Recall, for example, that some Hollenbeck working group members had assumed that gang violence, motivated by attempts by rival gangs to encroach upon and wrestle away control of the illicit drug market, was at the core of violence in the neighborhood, an assumption that turned out to be incorrect. A larger point here is not just that community representatives may sometimes be mistaken about the extent of broader problems, but that even within the same community different problems can require different approaches. Had research confirmed that drug retailing was indeed the cause of Hollenbeck violence, one plausible strategy for reducing violence might have been to disrupt the social interactions that dealers have with each other and with clients, or to increase area patrols and buy-and-bust actions so as to force drug markets indoors and break up street- or turf-based rivalries over drug markets.

While analysis of extant data can help document the exact nature of the violence problem to be addressed, in the same way analysis of homicide data helped pinpoint the nature of Hollenbeck gang violence, developing a complete intervention, particularly one with dynamic components, remains a difficult task. The LAPD, probation officers, and other partners from the criminal justice system were able to design an intervention with a powerful law enforcement component. Although the working group was equally committed to prevention and social intervention programs as part of the initiative, it had far fewer resources, or flexibility in these resources, to ensure widespread implementation of these services, much less a dynamic implementation that could change in response to the course of events.

We suspect that such intervention components will always lag behind law enforcement components unless extraordinary efforts are made to provide community-based organizations with the resources they need to become more effective partners in the interventions. Increasing investment in public education, providing more social services, increasing job opportunities, and implementing other programs that Angelenos suggest in community forums throughout the city can help reduce violence, but perhaps no more than they can help reduce other social ills such as teen pregnancy. Particularly in areas with more limited resources, broad prescriptions that attack root causes need to be combined with more focused efforts, especially law enforcement interventions, that promise more immediate effects.

BIBLIOGRAPHY

Barr, R., and K. Pease, "Crime Placement, Displacement and Deflection," in M. Tonry and N. Morris, eds., *Crime and Justice: A Review of Research*, Vol. 12, pp. 277–318, Chicago: University of Chicago Press, 1990.

Bartik, Timothy J., "Evaluating the Impacts of Local Economic Development Policies on Local Economic Outcomes: What Has Been Done and What Is Doable?" paper presented to the Conference on Evaluating Local Economic and Employment Development, Vienna, November 20, 2002.

Block, Carolyn R., and Richard L. Block, *Street Gang Crime in Chicago*, Washington, D.C.: U.S. Department of Justice, 1993.

Bondonio, Daniele, and John Engberg, "Enterprise Zones and Local Employment: Evidence from the States' Programs," *Regional Science and Urban Economics*, Vol. 30, No. 5, 2000, pp. 519–549.

Braga, Anthony A., David M. Kennedy, Elin J. Waring, and Anne Morrison Piehl, "Problem-Oriented Policing, Deterrence, and Youth Violence: An Evaluation of Boston's Operation Ceasefire," *Journal of Research in Crime and Delinquency*, Vol. 38, No. 3, August 2001, pp. 195–225.

Clarke, Rondald V., ed., *Situational Crime Prevention: Successful Case Studies*, New York: Harrow & Heston, 1992.

Cohen, Jacqueline, and George Tita, "Spatial Diffusion in Homicide: Exploring a General Method of Detecting Spatial Diffusion

Processes," *Journal of Quantitative Criminology*, Vol. 15, No. 4, December 1999, pp. 451–493.

Dehejia, Rajeev H., and Sadek Wahba, "Causal Effects in Non-experimental Studies: Reevaluating the Evaluation of Training Programs," *Journal of the American Statistical Association*, Vol. 94, No. 488, December 1999, pp. 1053–1062.

Engberg, John, and Robert Greenbaum, "State Enterprise Zones and Local Housing Markets," *Journal of Housing Research*, Vol. 10, No. 2, 1999, pp. 163–187.

Federal Bureau of Investigation, *Crime in the United States*, annual, available at http://www.fbi.gov/ucr/ucr.htm#cius (as of June 23, 2003).

Greenbaum, Robert, and John Engberg, "The Impact of State Urban Enterprise Zones on Business Outcomes," Washington, D.C.: U.S. Census Bureau Center for Economic Studies, Working Paper No. 98-20, 1998.

Greenbaum, Robert, and George Tita, "The Impact of Violence on Neighborhood Business Activity," paper presented at the Southern Regional Science Association's 41st Annual Meeting (Arlington, VA), NCOVR working paper YR4-SDRF4, April 2002.

Grogger, Jeffrey, "The Effects of Civil Gang Injunctions on Reported Violent Crime: Evidence from Los Angeles County," *Journal of Law and Economics*, Vol. 45, No. 1, April 2002, pp. 69–90.

Howell, James C., and Scott H. Decker, *The Gangs, Drugs, and Violence Connection*, Washington, D.C.: U.S. Department of Justice, 1999.

Kennedy, David M., "Pulling Levers: Chronic Offenders, High-Crime Settings, and a Theory of Prevention," *Valparaiso University Law Review*, Vol. 31, No. 2, Spring 1997, pp. 449–484.

Kennedy, David M., Anne M. Piehl, and Anthony A. Braga, "Youth Violence in Boston: Gun Markets, Serious Youth Offenders, and a Use-Reduction Strategy," *Law and Contemporary Problems*, Vol. 59, No. 1, Winter 1996, pp. 147–196.

Los Angeles Police Department, *Statistical Digest*, annual, available at http://www.lapdonline.org (as of June 23, 2003).

Maxson, Cheryl L., Karen Hennigan, and David C. Sloane, "For the Sake of the Neighborhood? Civil Gang Injunctions as a Gang Intervention Tool in Southern California," in Scott Decker, ed., *Policing Gangs and Youth Violence*, Belmont, Calif.: Wadsworth, 2003, pp. 239–266.

Maxson, Cheryl L., and Malcolm W. Klein, "Defining Gang Homicide: An Updated Look at Member and Motive Approaches," in *Gangs in America*, 2nd edition, C. Ronald Huff, ed., Newbury Park, Calif.: Sage Publications, 1996, pp. 3–20.

Moore, Joan W., *Homeboys: Gangs, Drugs, and Prison in the Barrios of Los Angeles*, Philadelphia: Temple University Press, 1978.

Rosenbaum, Paul R., and Donald B. Rubin, "The Central Role of the Propensity Score in Observational Studies for Causal Effects," *Biometrika*, Vol. 70, No. 1, April 1983, pp. 41–55.

Rosenbaum, Paul, and Donald B. Rubin, "Reducing the Bias in Observational Studies Using Subclassification on the Propensity Score," *Journal of the American Statistical Association*, Vol. 79, No. 387, September 1984, pp. 525–530.

Rosenfeld, Richard, Timothy M. Bray, and Arlen Egley, "Facilitating Violence: A Comparison of Gang-Motivated, Gang-Affiliated, and Nongang Youth Homicides," *Journal of Quantitative Criminology*, Vol. 15, No. 4, December 1999, pp. 495–516.

Tita, George, "Explaining Gang Crime: Social or Geographical Space?" paper presented at annual meeting of the American Society of Criminology, Chicago, November 2002.

Tita, George, and Elizabeth Griffiths, "Traveling to Violence: The Case for a Mobility-Based Spatial Typology of Homicide," Pittsburgh: Carnegie Mellon University, National Consortium on Violence Research Working Paper No. 03-07, 2003.

Tita, George, K. Jack Riley, and Peter Greenwood, "From Boston to Boyle Heights: The Process and Prospects of a 'Pulling Levers' Strategy in a Los Angeles Barrio," in Scott Decker, ed., *Policing*

Gangs and Youth Violence, Belmont, Calif.: Wadsworth, 2003, pp. 102–130.

Vigil, James Diego, *Barrio Gangs: Street Life and Identity in Southern California*, Austin: University of Texas Press, 1988.

Vigil, James Diego, "Cholos and Gangs: Culture Change and Street Youth in Los Angeles," in C. Ronald Huff, ed., *Gangs in America*, Newbury Park, Calif.: Sage Publications, 1990, pp. 116–128.

Vigil, James Diego, and Steve Chong Yun, "Vietnamese Youth Gangs in Southern California," in C. Ronald Huff, ed., *Gangs in America*, Newbury Park, Calif.: Sage Publications, 1990, pp. 146–162.